Web 3.0 for Beginners

How Blockchain, Decentralization, and Ownership Are Changing the Way We Live and Work

By Joe Correa

Published by Live Stronger Faster

First Edition

Table of Contents

Introduction

Web 3.0 is not a trend, a buzzword, or a passing moment in technology. It is a fundamental shift in how humanity organizes information, value, work, identity, and ownership on the internet. If Web 1.0 gave us information and Web 2.0 gave us social interaction, Web 3.0 gives us something far more powerful: the ability for everyday people—not corporations—to own digital assets, control their data, earn from their participation, and build lives, businesses, and wealth inside a global digital economy that operates 24/7. This introduction prepares you for that shift. It is designed to show you not only what Web 3.0 is, but why it matters, how it changes the way we live and work, and why those who understand and adopt this movement early will have an advantage as big as the early adopters of the internet, smartphones, YouTube, and the social media revolution.

To understand Web 3.0 properly, you must first recognize how dramatically the internet has evolved. In Web 1.0, we only consumed information—static websites, basic text, and limited interaction. We were spectators, not participants. Web 2.0 transformed us from spectators into creators, giving everyone the ability to post, share, like, comment, upload videos, and build platforms. But with this came a hidden cost: the largest companies controlled our data, dictated our visibility, profited from our attention, and used algorithms to influence what we saw, felt, and even believed. Web 3.0 emerges as a direct response to this imbalance. It flips the power structure. It gives ownership back to users. It transforms the internet into a decentralized ecosystem where anyone can earn, build, store value, and make decisions without relying on a central authority.

Blockchain is the technology that makes this possible. But contrary to common belief, blockchain is not just about cryptocurrencies. It is a ledger, a secure digital foundation that stores information in a transparent, tamper-resistant way. It's the infrastructure that allows you to prove ownership without needing a bank, an institution, or a corporation to validate it. It enables a digital identity that you control. It allows creators to sell digital art or music without platforms taking huge fees. It empowers gamers to sell in-game assets that once belonged only to studios. It allows everyday people to invest in digital real estate, participate in global organizations called DAOs, and earn passive income through staking, tokens, royalties, and decentralized apps. In Web 3.0, everything you own is actually yours.

But the heart of Web 3.0 goes beyond ownership—it is about participation. Instead of being a user who contributes value for free, you become a collaborator who earns value back. Instead of being the product, you become the shareholder. Every interaction—shopping, voting, learning, gaming, streaming, building, contributing—has the potential to generate income, rewards, influence, or assets. This is why Web 3.0 is often called the "Ownership Economy." It is the first time in human history where the everyday internet user can claim a direct economic stake in the platforms they help grow.

This shift does not only affect technology enthusiasts or crypto investors. It affects entrepreneurs, creators, businesses, employees, freelancers, gamers, educators, musicians, artists, athletes, real estate investors, and everyday people who simply want more freedom, opportunity, and financial control. It affects how companies hire and compensate talent, how communities form, how entertainment is created, how financial services operate, and how digital experiences are designed. The jobs of the future—blockchain strategists, Web3 designers, smart contract auditors, NFT community managers, token economists, virtual event creators, avatar designers—are already being filled across the globe. And many require no coding skills at all.

Three forces make Web 3.0 possible: decentralization, tokenization, and interoperability. Decentralization removes gatekeepers, allowing peer-to-peer interaction without relying on corporations. Tokenization transforms digital items—art, music, land, currencies, memberships, game items, access rights—into assets that can be owned, sold, transferred, or monetized. Interoperability connects these assets across platforms, meaning what you own in one world can be used in another. Combined, these forces create a fully integrated digital universe where value flows freely, transparently, and globally.

Web 3.0 also rewrites the rules of work. Instead of employment being tied to one company or one location, individuals participate in global ecosystems where contributions are measured and rewarded through tokens, royalties, on-chain proof, or decentralized reputation systems. A teenager in India can earn from play-to-earn games. A creator in Brazil can sell NFTs directly to a fan in France. A freelance designer can work inside a DAO and be paid automatically without invoices. A virtual builder can earn thousands designing digital storefronts or metaverse homes. Work becomes borderless. Talent becomes global. Income becomes digital and on demand.

This introduction also prepares you for the mindset shift required to navigate Web 3.0 safely and intelligently. It is normal to feel overwhelmed by the terminology—blockchain, tokens, wallets, smart contracts, decentralization, gas fees,

NFTs, DAOs, DeFi—but each of these concepts becomes simple when understood in the context of how they improve your digital life. Web 3.0 is not about memorizing jargon. It is about understanding the principles: you control your assets; you own your digital identity; you participate in networks that reward you; you unlock opportunities that did not exist before.

Most importantly, learning Web 3.0 now positions you ahead of the curve. Most of the world still hasn't understood—even slightly—how massive this transformation really is. They compare it to apps, websites, or social media. But Web 3.0 is much bigger. It is the next foundation of the global economy. It is the operating system of the metaverse. It is the structure behind decentralized finance. It is the new blueprint for work, creativity, community, and innovation. Just like early internet adopters built billion-dollar companies before the rest of the world realized what was happening, Web 3.0 early adopters will build the next generation of creators, investors, entrepreneurs, and digital pioneers.

This book will guide you through everything you need to confidently navigate Web 3.0, even if you are brand new to blockchain or crypto. You will understand why decentralization matters, how blockchain works, how digital wallets store value, how tokens unlock new opportunities, how decentralized apps function, how digital identity evolves, how ownership is verified, and how everyday people can use these systems to build income, careers, businesses, and long-term wealth. You will learn relevant examples, real-life use cases, and practical steps you can take immediately—even with zero technical background.

By the end of this book, you will not only understand Web 3.0—you will know how to move inside it. You will know where the opportunities are, what skills are valuable, what platforms matter, what risks to avoid, and how to position yourself as a knowledgeable participant in a world moving away from corporate control and toward decentralized ownership. This is your gateway into a new kind of internet—one where you are not just a user or observer, but an owner, creator, investor, and digital citizen.

Welcome to Web 3.0. Your future in the decentralized digital world begins now.

Chapter 1

Understanding Web 3.0: The Foundation of a Decentralized Internet

Web 3.0 is much more than an upgrade to the existing internet—it is a complete restructuring of how value, identity, ownership, and digital interaction operate online. To understand this transformation clearly, you must start with the core principles that define Web 3.0 and set it apart from the earlier versions of the internet. Web 1.0 was static and informational. Web 2.0 became interactive and social but centralized. Web 3.0 is decentralized, value-driven, and built on technologies that allow individuals to own their digital lives rather than renting them from platforms. This shift is not theoretical; it already powers financial systems, social platforms, communities, games, digital economies, and global organizations running without traditional corporate structures.

At the core of Web 3.0 is the idea of decentralization. In Web 2.0, a handful of companies control the majority of the internet's data, content, communication, algorithms, and economic value. Facebook decides what you see. Google decides what ranks. YouTube decides who gets visibility. Banks decide what transactions are allowed. App stores decide what can be published. Web 3.0 disrupts this entire hierarchy. It moves control from corporations into protocols—open systems governed by smart contracts, tokens, and communities that vote on decisions. In a decentralized network, no single company or authority can alter data, censor users at will, or shut down access. You become the owner of your assets, your interactions, and your identity.

The next foundational element of Web 3.0 is blockchain technology, the digital infrastructure that ensures transparency, security, and verification without needing an intermediary. Blockchain is a distributed ledger—a database stored across thousands of independent computers around the world. Every transaction, update, or piece of information added to the blockchain is validated by a network of participants and secured through cryptography. This makes it extremely difficult to alter, hack, or manipulate. The blockchain is not a single entity; there are many blockchains, such as Ethereum, Solana, Polygon, Avalanche, Cardano, and others. Each of these blockchains powers different ecosystems of apps, tokens, NFTs, and decentralized platforms.

Another pillar of Web 3.0 is digital ownership through tokens. A token can represent many things: currency, access, membership, rewards, rights, votes, or even physical property. Tokens allow people to participate in networks as stakeholders rather than passive users. For example, instead of using a social network for free while the platform sells your data, Web 3.0 platforms issue tokens to users, allowing them to benefit from the network's growth. NFTs (non-fungible tokens), a special type of token, represent unique items—art, music, virtual land, game assets, or digital identity collectibles. These tokens can be bought, sold, transferred, or used across platforms. For the first time, digital items behave like physical property.

Smart contracts are another breakthrough technology powering Web 3.0. A smart contract is a self-executing agreement that automatically performs actions when certain conditions are met. It requires no lawyers, no middlemen, and no manual verification. A simple example is paying for an online subscription: instead of a company charging your card monthly, a smart contract can automatically manage access rights and payments based on blockchain data. Smart contracts ensure transparency, reduce human error, prevent fraud, and make global interactions instant and programmable. Nearly every Web 3.0 platform relies on smart contracts to function.

Web 3.0 also transforms identity through the concept of self-sovereign identity. In Web 2.0, your identity belongs to the platforms you use. Your photos belong to Instagram. Your posts belong to Facebook. Your videos belong to YouTube. And your login credentials and personal data are stored in centralized servers that have repeatedly been hacked, leaked, or exploited. Web 3.0 gives you a digital wallet that acts as your identity. You own it. You control it. It cannot be taken away, suspended, or censored unless you choose to abandon it. This wallet connects to apps, stores assets, verifies ownership, and proves your participation—all without exposing your private data. You show what you want, when you want.

Another significant benefit of Web 3.0 is interoperability. In Web 2.0, platforms are isolated ecosystems. Your items in one game cannot be used in another. Your social platform identity does not transfer. Your data stays locked inside each site. Web 3.0 breaks these walls. It creates a fluid digital environment where assets, identity, and interactions can move across platforms without friction. For example, your avatar skin purchased on one platform could be used inside a different metaverse world. Your NFT membership could unlock access to multiple apps, communities, or virtual events. Interoperability unlocks massive value because it makes digital ownership portable and universal.

Decentralized applications, or dApps, are the user-facing layer of Web 3.0. They look and operate like regular apps, but instead of running on centralized servers, they run on blockchain networks. This means they are transparent, resistant to censorship, and governed by community decisions. Examples include decentralized finance platforms (DeFi), play-to-earn games, metaverse worlds, decentralized social networks, NFT marketplaces, and DAO management tools. Many dApps allow users to earn rewards for providing value—such as lending, trading, creating content, or participating in governance.

Understanding Web 3.0 also requires understanding DAOs—Decentralized Autonomous Organizations. A DAO is an online community that makes decisions collectively through token-based voting. There is no CEO, no headquarters, and no hierarchy. Instead, members propose ideas, vote on actions, and fund initiatives using a shared treasury. Thousands of DAOs exist today, managing billions of dollars across creator communities, investment clubs, protocol governance groups, charity initiatives, and metaverse projects. DAOs represent the future of online organizations and redefine how groups coordinate globally.

Finally, the economic layer of Web 3.0 revolutionizes how people earn money online. People can earn through staking, farming, providing liquidity, play-to-earn games, participating in governance, selling NFTs, contributing to DAOs, freelancing in Web3 jobs, or building digital property in the metaverse.

This new digital economy rewards participation, creativity, ownership, and early adoption. It removes traditional barriers, giving global opportunities to anyone with an internet connection.

By understanding these foundational concepts, you are now prepared to move deeper into the Web 3.0 world. The chapters ahead will break down each element—wallets, tokens, NFTs, DeFi, DAOs, decentralized identity, metaverse economies, and investment opportunities—so you can navigate Web 3.0 confidently and profitably. You are entering a new era of the internet—one built for owners.

"The Key to the Third Internet"

Alex never imagined the internet could surprise him again. He had lived through the early days of dial-up, the rise of Google and Facebook, the explosion of mobile apps, and the era where influencers became celebrities from their bedrooms. But the night he stumbled into the Web 3.0 world, everything he thought he understood about the internet changed.

It started with a message from his younger cousin, Mateo. "Bro, download this wallet. I'll show you something crazy." Alex almost ignored it; he had heard enough about crypto scams, NFTs, and digital coins that sounded like jokes. But something about Mateo's excitement felt different. He clicked the link, installed the app, and within seconds, a long string of numbers and letters appeared on his screen. "Welcome to your new identity," Mateo said through a voice note. "That right there is your key to the third version of the internet."

Alex laughed. "A bunch of numbers? That's my identity?" Mateo replied instantly. "It's more than that. It's the first thing online that actually belongs to you."

Curiosity took over. Alex asked what he should do next, and Mateo told him to join a Web 3.0 community call that was starting in five minutes. Alex hesitated—he wasn't dressed, he looked tired, and he didn't know anything about blockchain—but he joined anyway. The host, a woman named Rhea, welcomed hundreds of people from dozens of countries: artists from Brazil, gamers from Korea, investors from Dubai, college students from the U.S., and even retirees exploring new hobbies. Rhea began by explaining what Alex had never realized: that for decades, he had been renting his digital life.

Every photo he posted, every message he wrote, every video he uploaded—all of it belonged to the platforms, not him. They used his data to grow, profit, and influence the world while he received nothing in return. "Web 3.0 changes the power structure," Rhea said. "It gives you ownership over your identity, your assets, your work, your creativity, and your place in the digital economy."

As she spoke, Alex felt a strange mix of shock and excitement. He had always known companies collected data, but he never understood the scale. He never realized how little control he actually had. Rhea continued, explaining blockchain, tokens, wallets, and DAOs in simple terms. The chat filled with questions, links, and people sharing their first experiences in Web 3.0. Mateo messaged privately: "See? This is what I've been telling you. People are building the next internet."

At the end of the call, Rhea told everyone to check their wallets. Alex refreshed his and gasped. A small token appeared—his first digital asset. Not worth much, maybe a few cents, but it was symbolic. "That token," Rhea said, "is your proof of participation. It shows you were here. It belongs to you. No one can delete it, freeze it, or take it away."

Alex stayed up half the night learning more. He discovered decentralized apps that didn't rely on companies, marketplaces where artists kept full ownership of their work, games where players truly owned their items, and communities where decisions were made by token holders rather than CEOs. He even found an online group building a virtual city in the metaverse—every building owned by its contributors.

By sunrise, he felt something he hadn't felt since he was a kid exploring the internet for the first time: wonder. For years, technology felt predictable, controlled, repetitive. But Web 3.0 felt alive. It felt open. It felt like the early internet he had once loved—except this time, users weren't just spectators. They were owners.

A few days later, Mateo sent him another message: "You ready for your first DAO vote?" Alex blinked. "Vote? On what?" Mateo replied with a smiley face. "On the future of the project you just joined."

When Alex opened the voting platform, he stared at the proposals. People from around the world were deciding how to use the group's treasury, which tools to build next, and which creators to fund. His vote mattered. His token gave him a voice. It was the first time he felt like the internet wasn't something being done *to him*, but something he could help shape.

In that moment, Alex understood what the next version of the internet truly was. Not a collection of apps, not a trend, and not a speculative bubble. It was a system built on ownership, participation, transparency, and collective creation. A place where he—an ordinary guy—could have influence, identity, and assets that couldn't be taken away.

The internet had evolved. And now, so had he.

Chapter 2

Digital Wallets: Your Identity, Bank, and Passport in Web 3.0

A digital wallet is the most important tool in Web 3.0. It is your identity, your storage vault, your access key, your authentication system, and your financial hub. If Web 2.0 accounts are usernames and passwords stored on corporate servers, Web 3.0 wallets are decentralized identities that exist only under your control. Understanding wallets is essential because every action in the decentralized internet flows through them: holding tokens, buying NFTs, accessing metaverse platforms, voting in DAOs, logging into decentralized apps, and proving ownership. Without a wallet, there is no meaningful participation in Web 3.0.

A digital wallet is not like a physical wallet that stores cash. Instead, it stores private keys—special cryptographic codes that give you control over your digital assets. The blockchain does not store your coins inside your wallet; it records that you are the owner. Your wallet connects to this record using private keys, proving your ownership. Whoever controls the private keys controls the assets. This concept is revolutionary because it removes intermediaries. There is no bank to freeze your account, no platform to close your profile, no company to seize your balance. Your wallet is your sovereign identity, and its security depends entirely on how you manage it.

There are two major categories of wallets: custodial and non-custodial. Custodial wallets are managed by companies (like exchanges), meaning they hold your keys for you. These wallets are beginner-friendly but do not give you full ownership because the company has ultimate control. Non-custodial wallets, on the other hand, give you full self-custody. You control your keys, your assets, and your access. No one can take them, freeze them, or modify them. For anyone serious about Web 3.0, non-custodial wallets are essential. They empower true ownership, independence, and decentralized participation.

Understanding public and private keys is also fundamental. Your public key is like a username—something you can share to receive tokens, NFTs, or digital assets. Your private key is more like the master password to your entire digital life. You must never share it with anyone. To make wallets easier to use, private keys are often represented as a "seed phrase"—usually 12 or 24 random words. This phrase is the backup for your identity. If you lose access to your device, you can restore your wallet using the seed phrase anywhere in the world. If someone else gains access to your seed phrase, they can take everything you own. This is why Web 3.0 wallets require a new level of responsibility and awareness.

Another important concept is wallet types. The most common are browser extension wallets (like MetaMask), mobile wallets (like Coinbase Wallet or Trust Wallet), and hardware wallets (like Ledger or Trezor). Browser wallets are ideal for connecting with decentralized apps on your computer. Mobile wallets are convenient for daily use, QR scanning, and portable access. Hardware wallets are physical devices that store your private keys offline, making them nearly impossible to hack. For large holdings or long-term storage, hardware wallets are the gold standard.

Wallets also interact with different blockchain networks. Unlike Web 2.0 platforms that operate independently, Web 3.0 requires wallets capable of switching between blockchains such as Ethereum, Polygon, Solana, Avalanche, Binance Smart Chain, and others. Many wallets support multiple networks, allowing users to manage assets across various ecosystems with a single interface. Understanding how networks work—and ensuring transactions occur on the correct network—is a critical skill for avoiding mistakes and unnecessary costs.

Digital wallets also perform powerful functions beyond storage. They allow you to sign transactions, which is the process that authorizes actions on the blockchain. Signing can mean approving a purchase, confirming a trade, accessing a metaverse world, logging into a dApp, or voting in a DAO. Unlike Web 2.0 logins that rely on passwords stored in corporate databases, Web 3.0 wallets authenticate you cryptographically, eliminating the need for personal data sharing. When you connect your wallet to a platform, you are proving "I am the owner of this address" without revealing your identity. This approach enhances privacy, security, and independence.

Another transformative feature of wallets is the ability to hold and manage NFTs. Because NFTs have many use cases—from art and collectibles to identity passes and game assets—wallets act as your display case, membership cardholder, and inventory manager. Your wallet can contain digital land deeds, avatar wearables, metaverse tickets, certifications, licenses, or earned rewards. This makes wallets central to your digital presence, not just your financial activity.

Security is a crucial part of understanding wallets. Because you control your own keys, you must protect them. This means storing seed phrases safely offline, avoiding screenshots, never entering recovery phrases on random websites, and using hardware wallets for significant assets. Most Web 3.0 scams succeed not because blockchains are insecure, but because users unknowingly authorize malicious transactions or expose their seed phrases. Proper wallet security transforms Web 3.0 from a risky environment into a powerful system of freedom and opportunity.

Finally, wallets enable financial activities in decentralized finance (DeFi). They allow you to lend, borrow, stake, earn interest, trade without intermediaries, or participate in liquidity pools. In Web 2.0, these functions require banks or financial institutions. In Web 3.0, your wallet becomes your bank—global, borderless, permissionless, and always open. You can earn yield from blockchain protocols, pay zero intermediaries, and engage in financial activities with transparency and independence.

In summary, the digital wallet is the foundation of your Web 3.0 journey. It is your key, your vault, your login, your identity, your access, and your freedom. Mastering wallets is the first step to becoming a fully capable participant in the decentralized internet.

"The Wallet That Opened a New World"

Sophia had always been fascinated by technology, but she never considered herself an expert. She used social media, streamed movies, bought things online, and worked remotely, but the deeper layers of the internet were a mystery to her. That changed the night she discovered digital wallets. It was a discovery that felt less like downloading an app and more like unlocking a door she never knew existed.

The journey began when her friend Luca invited her to a Web 3.0 workshop. Sophia almost didn't go—she assumed the event would be filled with crypto enthusiasts and jargon she wouldn't understand. But curiosity won. When she arrived, the room was filled with ordinary people: teachers, artists, business owners, students, and retirees. Luca whispered, "This isn't about crypto—it's about the future."

The instructor, a woman named Zara, began by asking everyone to hold up their phones. "This," Zara said, "is your window into the digital world. But tonight, we're going to give your phone something new: a wallet that belongs fully to you." Sophia watched as Zara walked them through the steps. They downloaded a non-custodial wallet, created a new identity, and were presented with a set of random words—their seed phrase. Zara paused and looked at them seriously. "These words," she said, "are the keys to your digital life. Guard them like your most valuable possession." Sophia wrote hers carefully, feeling a weight she couldn't explain.

As the workshop continued, Zara explained that this wallet was not just for money—it was for ownership. "Your photos, your identity, your memberships, your assets... in Web 3.0, all of it can live here. And no company can take it away from you." That idea hit Sophia hard. She remembered losing her previous Instagram account to a random suspension she couldn't appeal. She remembered her bank freezing her card during a trip, claiming it was for "security." She remembered apps that locked her out after glitchy updates. For the first time, she understood how little control she actually had.

Zara had them connect their wallets to a decentralized app. With a single tap, Sophia watched as her wallet authenticated her identity—no email, no password, no verification code. The app simply recognized her. It felt surreal. "You just logged in without giving away your data," Zara said proudly. "That is the power of cryptographic identity." Sophia felt like she had stepped into a new internet, one where she existed without needing permission.

Then something unexpected happened. Zara smiled and told everyone to check their wallets. A small NFT had appeared—an attendance badge minted on the blockchain. It wasn't fancy or valuable, just a digital token proving she had completed the workshop. But for Sophia, it felt like receiving her first passport stamp. It was proof that she belonged somewhere new.

After the session, Luca showed Sophia how NFTs could represent art, event tickets, game items, or even certifications. He explained how wallets could connect to virtual worlds and control avatars. He demonstrated how decentralized finance apps let people lend and borrow money without banks. He even told her about DAOs—online communities where people like her could vote on decisions. Every new concept widened her eyes. Every example revealed opportunities she never knew existed.

At one point, Luca asked, “Do you see what’s happening?” Sophia nodded slowly. “It’s like we’ve been living in someone else’s house this whole time,” she said, “and tonight I got the keys to my own place.” She felt empowered in a way she had never experienced online before.

Over the next week, Sophia explored more apps using her wallet. She bought her first NFT, joined a DAO’s beginner community, and even experimented with a small amount of cryptocurrency to understand transactions. Each action required her approval. Each win felt like progress. Each mistake taught her something new. The more she learned, the more she realized the wallet wasn't just a tool—it was a symbol of independence.

One night, while sitting on her balcony, she opened her wallet app and stared at the assets inside it. They weren't worth much yet—some tokens, a membership NFT, and a badge from her workshop. But they were hers. No platform could delete them. No company could freeze them. No password reset could wipe them away. She imagined a future where digital property behaved the same way physical property did—where she could own her online presence without compromise.

As she closed the app, she whispered to herself, "This is just the beginning." And she was right. The wallet had opened a door to a world she didn't even know she was missing. A world where she wasn't just a user trapped in platforms, but a citizen of a decentralized universe she could help shape.

Chapter 3

Understanding Blockchain: The Technology Powering Web 3.0

Blockchain is the backbone of Web 3.0. While terms like crypto, NFTs, metaverse, tokens, and decentralization often receive the most attention, none of them would exist without blockchain technology. To understand Web 3.0 as a whole, you must first understand what blockchain is, why it matters, and how it solves problems traditional internet systems have never been able to overcome. Blockchain is not complicated—it is simply different. And those who grasp its fundamentals gain an immediate advantage in navigating the future of the digital world.

At its core, a blockchain is a distributed ledger—a digital record of transactions, data, or actions that is stored across thousands of computers rather than one centralized server. In traditional Web 2.0 systems, your information sits inside databases owned by companies. If a company is hacked, corrupted, or shut down, your data is vulnerable. Blockchain removes this risk by storing identical copies of the ledger across a decentralized network of independent nodes. Each node verifies what happens on the chain, ensuring accuracy and preventing manipulation. No single entity—no government, corporation, or platform—can alter the records without consensus from the network. This is what makes blockchain trustworthy, transparent, and unstoppable.

One of the most important concepts to understand is immutability. When data is added to a blockchain, it cannot be changed or deleted without altering every subsequent block—a nearly impossible task. This creates a permanent digital trail that increases trust, accountability, and security. Whether it's a financial transaction, property deed, identity record, vote, or membership, the blockchain preserves the exact history forever. Immutability also eliminates fraud and tampering. In a world where digital manipulation is easy, blockchain brings mathematical certainty and verifiable truth.

Blockchain operates through a system of blocks and chains. Each block contains data—transactions, interactions, or updates—and a cryptographic link to the block before it. These links create a chain, forming an unbreakable sequence of information. New blocks are added through consensus mechanisms, the most common being Proof of Work (used by Bitcoin) and Proof of Stake (used by Ethereum). In Proof of Work, miners compete to solve mathematical puzzles, securing the network but using large amounts of energy. In Proof of Stake, validators lock up tokens as collateral and are chosen to create blocks based on their stake. Proof of Stake is faster, more efficient, and environmentally friendly, which is why many modern blockchains use it.

Blockchain is not a single technology—there are thousands of blockchains, each with unique strengths and ecosystems. Ethereum is known for smart contracts and decentralized apps. Bitcoin focuses on decentralized money. Solana emphasizes speed and low fees. Polygon improves Ethereum's scalability. Avalanche, Algorand, Near, Cardano, and others bring their own innovations. These blockchains form the foundations of Web 3.0 platforms, games, metaverse worlds, NFT markets, and decentralized finance systems. Understanding differences between chains helps you choose where to participate, invest, or build.

Smart contracts are another essential part of blockchain functionality. A smart contract is a piece of code that automatically executes actions when certain conditions are met. It replaces middlemen, lawyers, and manual verification. For example, if someone buys your NFT, the smart contract automatically transfers ownership and sends you payment. If a DAO votes on a proposal, the smart contract executes the decision without human bias. Smart contracts power everything from financial protocols to loyalty programs, membership passes, rental agreements, and automated payouts. They are unbiased, transparent, and reliable.

Blockchain's transparency is another powerful feature. While the identities of users can remain private, the transactions themselves are visible to everyone. This creates an open-source economy where anyone can verify what is happening. In Web 2.0, companies hide their systems behind closed servers. In Web 3.0, the logic is public. Anyone can inspect the code, monitor transactions, analyze flows of capital, or see the history of an asset. Transparency creates trust at scale and allows people to participate without needing blind faith in an institution.

Security is a natural benefit of blockchain architecture. Because the ledger is distributed across thousands of nodes, hackers cannot simply attack one database. They would need to compromise a majority of the network simultaneously—an unrealistic task on large blockchains like Bitcoin or Ethereum. This makes blockchain one of the safest systems ever created. In fact, most "crypto hacks" stem from user error—giving away seed phrases, signing malicious transactions, or interacting with fraudulent websites—not from vulnerabilities in blockchain technology itself.

Understanding why blockchain matters requires understanding the problems it solves. In traditional systems, ownership is fragile. Platforms can freeze accounts, governments can restrict transfers, banks can decline transactions, and companies can lose your data. With blockchain, ownership becomes absolute. You hold assets in your wallet. You control access. No institution can reverse, freeze, or litigate your digital property. This level of sovereignty is revolutionary and forms the basis of the Web 3.0 ownership economy.

Blockchain also democratizes participation. Anyone with internet access can join a blockchain network, earn tokens, contribute to a DAO, vote in governance, mint NFTs, or build a business. There are no borders, no credit checks, no approvals, and no gatekeepers. The barriers that once restricted financial opportunity and global collaboration disappear completely. This is why blockchain is spreading rapidly across communities, industries, and countries.

Interoperability is the next phase of blockchain evolution. Instead of isolated ecosystems, new technologies allow blockchains to communicate and exchange data. This will create a fully interconnected digital world where assets can move smoothly across platforms. Imagine buying an item in one game and using it in another, or borrowing money on one chain and paying back on another. Interoperability turns blockchain networks into a global economic web.

In summary, blockchain is the technological foundation that enables Web 3.0 to exist. It introduces decentralization, transparency, trust, automation, and digital sovereignty at a global scale. Understanding blockchain is not optional—it is essential for anyone who wants to navigate, invest, work, or build inside the decentralized future.

"Blocks in the Ledger of Tomorrow"

Elias had heard the word "blockchain" for years, usually in conversations he didn't understand: crypto investors bragging about profits, news anchors discussing digital currencies, influencers promoting NFT collections. But none of it clicked. It all felt like noise—until the day he visited his uncle Arturo's small workshop. Arturo was a retired engineer, the type who still built gadgets for fun and kept a whiteboard full of equations even in retirement. When Elias mentioned he was trying to understand Web 3.0, Arturo's eyes lit up.

"You need to see something," Arturo said. He took Elias to his cluttered desk and opened a program on his computer. "This," he said, pointing to rows of data scrolling down the screen, "is a live blockchain explorer. Every line you see is a transaction happening somewhere in the world." Elias leaned closer. It looked like a waterfall of code. "But... what's actually happening?" he asked. Arturo smiled. "The next version of the internet is writing itself." Arturo explained that each line represented someone sending value, minting an NFT, deploying a smart contract, or interacting with a decentralized app. “All of this,” Arturo said, “is being recorded permanently across thousands of computers. No one can alter it. No one can hide it. No one owns it. And that,” he continued, tapping the screen, “is what makes Web 3.0 possible.” Elias felt a spark he hadn’t felt since he was a child taking apart his toys just to see how they worked.

Over the next hour, Arturo broke down the concept of blockchain in the simplest possible terms. “Imagine a notebook,” he said. “But instead of one person writing in it, millions of people are writing in identical copies at the same time. And before anything new gets written, everyone agrees it’s valid.” Elias began to visualize it—pages added one after another, each page linked to the previous one with unbreakable glue. “That’s why it’s called a block and chain,” Arturo finished.

To make the idea more concrete, Arturo pulled up a diagram showing decentralized nodes. “In Web 2.0,” he explained, “your information lives on servers owned by companies. If those servers fail—or get hacked—your data is at risk. But on a blockchain, your data lives everywhere and nowhere at the same time. Every node stores a copy. So even if half the network disappeared, your information would still exist.” Elias felt the weight of that realization. The fragility of traditional internet systems suddenly became obvious. Then Arturo opened a smart contract. The lines of code looked intimidating, but the function was simple. "This," Arturo said, "is an agreement between strangers that will execute itself without anyone enforcing it." He showed Elias an example: a contract that automatically released payment when digital art was sold. "There's no bank, no platform, no person who gets in the way," Arturo said. "Just math." Elias felt a shiver run through him. The world he knew—full of intermediaries, approvals, and waiting—felt suddenly outdated.

As the evening continued, Arturo told stories of people around the world using blockchain for everyday life. Farmers in Africa tracking their crops. Artists minting their work and earning full ownership. Developers building virtual worlds. Communities voting in DAOs. Even entire cities experimenting with blockchain-based public records. Elias realized blockchain wasn't about hype—it was about creating a system people could trust without relying on institutions.

At one point, Arturo turned to him and said, "This technology will outlive us all. Everything you record on a blockchain becomes part of a permanent history." That sentence stayed with Elias. In a world where misinformation spread easily and digital content vanished overnight, the idea of a permanent, verifiable record felt comforting. Before leaving the workshop, Arturo said one last thing: "Most people think blockchain is about money. They're wrong. It's about truth." Elias walked home that night under the glow of streetlights, replaying the day's lessons in his mind. The streets looked the same, but the world felt different. He imagined blockchains humming beneath the surface of daily life—silent, precise, incorruptible.

Later, as he lay in bed, he opened a blockchain explorer on his phone. The same waterfall of transactions flowed across his screen. But this time, he didn't see code. He saw stories. Someone minting their first NFT. Someone joining a DAO. Someone transferring savings to a secure digital wallet. Someone interacting with a game. Someone funding a project. Someone adding a tiny block to humanity's shared ledger.

For the first time, Elias understood the technology that would shape the rest of his life. And he felt ready for it.

Chapter 4

Smart Contracts: The Automated Agreements That Run Web 3.0

Smart contracts are one of the most revolutionary components of Web 3.0, forming the foundation upon which decentralized applications, NFTs, DAOs, and metaverse interactions are built. While the term "smart contract" might sound complex or intimidating, the concept is surprisingly simple. A smart contract is a programmable agreement that automatically executes actions when predetermined conditions are met. It functions without lawyers, brokers, banks, or middlemen. Instead, it uses code to enforce rules, manage transactions, and ensure trust—all without requiring human intervention. This removes friction, delays, corruption, and costs that are prevalent in traditional systems.

To understand smart contracts clearly, imagine a vending machine. When you insert payment and select a product, the machine automatically dispenses your item. There is no cashier, no negotiation, and no oversight required. A smart contract works the same way. If certain conditions are fulfilled—such as sending a payment, reaching a deadline, or meeting a performance metric—the contract executes the agreed action instantly. This automation ensures fairness, transparency, and predictability, making smart contracts a fundamental upgrade to how digital agreements are created and enforced.

Smart contracts live on blockchains like Ethereum, Solana, Avalanche, Binance Smart Chain, Aptos, or Polygon. Once deployed, they cannot be changed without community consensus or a specific upgrade mechanism built into the code. This immutability creates trust. Because the contract's code is visible to anyone, users can verify exactly what a smart contract will do before interacting with it. There is no hidden fine print, no secret algorithms, and no manipulative terms. Everything is transparent, open, and verifiable. This is one of the primary reasons Web 3.0 has been celebrated as a fairer and more community-driven digital environment.

The logic inside smart contracts is written in programming languages tailored for blockchain development—such as Solidity (Ethereum), Rust (Solana), or Move (Aptos). However, you do not need to know how to code to use smart contracts. Most Web 3.0 platforms provide user-friendly interfaces that allow you to interact with contracts effortlessly. When you mint an NFT, stake assets, lend tokens, purchase virtual land, join a DAO, or perform any other on-chain action, you are interacting with a smart contract behind the scenes.

Every click you make sends instructions to the contract, which then performs the action automatically.

One of the most transformative aspects of smart contracts is the elimination of intermediaries. For centuries, contracts required trust in a third party—banks, lawyers, brokers, escrow agents, or corporations—to enforce terms. These intermediaries slowed down processes, increased costs, and introduced human error or bias. Smart contracts replace all of that with deterministic logic. The code cannot be bribed, biased, intimidated, or manipulated. It executes exactly as written. This creates a global environment where individuals, strangers, businesses, and organizations can interact securely without needing to trust each other personally.

Smart contracts also enable composability, meaning multiple contracts and decentralized applications can work together like digital building blocks. For example, one contract might manage identity, another might handle payments, another might verify ownership, and another might manage voting rights. These components can connect effortlessly because blockchain logic is open-source and interoperable. Composability accelerates innovation. Instead of building everything from scratch, developers can combine existing smart contracts to create new platforms—much like developers built early Web 2.0 apps by combining APIs from Google

Maps, YouTube, PayPal, and social networks. Many industries are being transformed by smart contracts. In finance, decentralized lending platforms use smart contracts to allow users to borrow or earn interest without banks. In real estate, smart contracts can handle digital deeds, rental agreements, or fractional property ownership. In supply chains, they track goods from manufacturing to delivery with transparency and zero fraud. In gaming, smart contracts govern digital assets, ownership rights, and in-game economies. In entertainment, they automate royalties for creators. In corporate governance, DAOs use smart contracts to manage voting, transparency, treasury spending, and collective decision-making.

NFTs, one of the most visible creations of Web 3.0, are entirely driven by smart contracts. When you mint an NFT, the smart contract registers the artwork, assigns ownership, and defines resale royalties. When an NFT is transferred, the contract updates the ownership record. When it is sold on a marketplace, the contract handles payment distribution automatically. This guarantees artists and creators receive fair compensation without relying on platforms or agents.

One of the most important characteristics of smart contracts is transparency. Unlike traditional contracts that are stored in private databases or physical files, smart contracts are visible to everyone on the blockchain. Anyone can inspect the logic, verify the rules, track updates, or monitor interactions. This creates a trustless environment, meaning trust is placed in code rather than institutions or individuals. Transparency also reduces corruption, fraud, and unauthorized changes.

However, smart contracts also come with responsibilities. Because they are immutable, poorly written contracts can cause problems if they contain bugs or vulnerabilities. To prevent this, major smart contracts undergo audits by cybersecurity firms that specialize in blockchain code. These audits ensure the contract behaves safely and predictably. Users should always interact with reputable platforms whose contracts have been audited. Understanding this best practice keeps you safe and confident when navigating the decentralized world.

In summary, smart contracts form the foundation of every decentralized application and service inside Web 3.0. They automate trust, enforce agreements, manage assets, and allow global systems to operate without centralized control. They are the silent engines powering nearly every innovation in the new internet. By understanding how they work, you gain insight into the core mechanisms that make Web 3.0 efficient, secure, and revolutionary.

"The Contract That Needed No Signature"

Maya had always been skeptical of anything involving the blockchain. Crypto felt too volatile, NFTs seemed strange, and the metaverse sounded like science fiction. But everything changed the day she needed to send money to her sister, Nina, who lived halfway across the world. The bank told her the transfer would take three to five days. The fees were outrageous. The process was slow. And Maya felt powerless. She wished there was a simpler, faster, fairer way.

The next morning, Maya met with her coworker Theo, who had been gently nudging her into learning about Web 3.0 for months. When she explained her frustration, Theo grinned and said, "I think it's time you learned about smart contracts." Maya rolled her eyes. "I'm not trying to get into crypto," she said. "I just need to help my sister." Theo leaned in. "Exactly. And smart contracts can do that—and much more." Something in his tone made her pause.

He pulled out his laptop and opened a decentralized finance app. "This," he said, "is powered by a smart contract. No bank. No delays. No permission. Just code." He showed Maya how he could send money instantly to anyone in the world. No forms. No waiting. No approvals. The platform simply asked him to confirm the transaction, and within seconds, the funds were delivered. Maya stared at the screen in disbelief. "That's it?" she said. Theo nodded. "That's it. The contract executed automatically."

Her curiosity awakened. "How does the contract know what to do?" she asked. Theo explained smart contracts in simple terms—agreements written in code, stored on the blockchain, executing themselves when certain conditions are met. "They don't need trust," he said. "Only logic." He showed her examples: a contract that triggered rent payments every month, a contract that shared music royalties instantly, a contract that released event tickets automatically when a QR code was scanned. Each example made Maya realize how many middlemen controlled everyday life.

Wanting to understand more, Maya agreed to watch a short live demonstration Theo was hosting that afternoon. When she joined the virtual event, she saw dozens of participants from around the world. Theo began by presenting a simple smart contract that validated donations for a charity. Every time someone contributed, the contract instantly updated the total and sent funds directly to the organization's wallet. No staff, no delays, no opportunity for funds to be "lost." The transparency stunned Maya. Every transaction was visible, verifiable, and permanent.

The moment that changed everything came when Theo displayed the code behind the contract. It wasn't pretty, but it wasn't mystical either. "Here is the agreement," he explained. "It says: if a user sends a donation to this address, the contract forwards it immediately. That's all." He highlighted each line, explaining that no person could interfere with the process—not even him. "It will run exactly like this forever," he said. "No one can alter it. That's the power of smart contracts."

As Maya listened, something clicked. She realized how much trust she had placed in institutions her whole life. She trusted banks to hold her money, landlords to honor agreements, agencies to process documents, and platforms to pay creators. But she also remembered the times she had been disappointed: delayed payments, lost paperwork, unfair fees, unexplained freezes. The idea that a simple piece of code could eliminate all of that felt both thrilling and terrifying.

That night, she decided to try it for herself. Following Theo's instructions, she used a smart-contract-based platform to send money to her sister. The process took less than a minute. Nina replied instantly: "How did you do that so fast?!" Maya smiled, feeling like she had discovered a cheat code for the world.

Over the next few weeks, Maya explored more smart contract applications. She joined a DAO where members voted on community improvements by interacting with contracts. She bought a digital event ticket that unlocked access automatically when her wallet connected. She even experimented with a small NFT purchase and watched as the smart contract transferred ownership instantly and flawlessly. One evening, Maya sat on her balcony watching the sunset when her phone vibrated. It was a notification from one of the platforms she was using. The smart contract had just distributed monthly rewards to all participants—including her. She hadn't lifted a finger. The code simply did its job, exactly as promised.

She stared at the message, feeling a mixture of humility and empowerment. For years, she believed that only institutions could manage rules, agreements, and transactions. Now she had seen a different world—one where fair systems operated without bias, delay, or corruption. Systems governed not by people, but by mathematics.

"The contract needed no signature," she whispered to herself. "Just truth."

And for the first time in her life, she felt like the digital world was finally working for her instead of against her.

Chapter 5

Tokens & Cryptocurrencies: The Fuel of the Decentralized Economy

Tokens and cryptocurrencies are the lifeblood of Web 3.0. Without them, decentralized systems would have no way to operate, reward participants, secure networks, or economically sustain platforms without relying on corporations. To understand Web 3.0 fully, you must understand tokens—not as speculative assets or gambling chips, but as digital building blocks that store value, represent ownership, enable utility, transfer rights, and allow global participation without middlemen. Tokens power decentralized finance, gaming, social platforms, metaverse worlds, DAOs, rewards systems, and every economic layer of the emerging decentralized internet.

A token is simply a digital asset recorded on a blockchain. But unlike traditional digital items, tokens are verifiable, portable, and immutable. They can represent currency, voting power, property rights, memberships, digital collectibles, or even identity attributes. Cryptocurrency is a type of token designed to function as money—borderless, programmable, secure, and independent of governments or banks. Bitcoin, Ethereum, Solana, and many others serve as digital currencies that can move across the world in seconds. But cryptocurrencies are only one category of tokens. Web 3.0 includes many forms, each with unique purposes.

There are four major categories of tokens in Web 3.0: **cryptocurrencies, utility tokens, governance tokens, and non-fungible tokens (NFTs).** Cryptocurrencies act as digital cash or store of value. They allow people to buy, sell, trade, and save without relying on traditional banks. Utility tokens power decentralized apps by enabling access, paying fees, or fueling smart contract execution. Governance tokens allow holders to vote on decisions, influence platforms, and participate in decentralized governance. NFTs represent unique digital assets such as art, music, virtual land, game items, identity credentials, or collectible artifacts. These categories give tokens flexibility far beyond the limits of physical currency.

Many blockchains also provide native tokens. For example, ETH is the native token of Ethereum, used to pay for transactions and smart contract execution (known as gas fees). SOL is the native token of Solana. MATIC is used on Polygon. AVAX powers the Avalanche network. These native tokens ensure the blockchain operates smoothly and securely. Validators or miners are rewarded with tokens for confirming transactions, maintaining the network, and securing the blockchain. This system creates an economy where participants are incentivized to support and strengthen decentralized infrastructure.

Utility tokens provide another layer of functionality. They allow users to access services, participate in ecosystems, unlock premium features, or perform certain actions within a platform. For example, utility tokens might be required to mint NFTs, buy metaverse land, join an online club, stake assets in DeFi pools, or access token-gated experiences. Utility tokens can be thought of as digital “fuel” that powers software, communities, games, and decentralized applications. They are essential for scalable, self-sustaining digital economies.

Governance tokens are central to decentralized decision-making. Instead of a CEO or board controlling a platform, governance token holders vote collectively. A user may propose updates, changes, funding allocations, or community initiatives. Each token typically equates to one vote. This ensures power is distributed across participants rather than centralized. DAOs rely heavily on governance tokens to manage treasuries, approve projects, reward contributors, and align incentives. Governance tokens transform users from consumers into stakeholders with a direct impact on the direction of a platform. NFTs represent the most creative category of tokens. While NFTs became famous for digital art, their true potential is far greater. An NFT can represent proof of attendance, proof of identity, certifications, game characters, membership cards, loyalty rewards, metaverse property, access passes, and more. NFTs also enable creators to earn royalties automatically through smart contracts. Every time their work is resold, the original artist receives a percentage—something nearly impossible in the traditional world. NFTs make digital ownership legitimate, transferable, and economically significant.

An essential concept in tokenization is **fungibility**. Fungible tokens like ETH or BTC are identical and interchangeable—similar to dollars. Non-fungible tokens (NFTs) are completely unique. You can trade fungible tokens equally, but each NFT has its own distinct value and identity. This distinction makes tokens versatile, allowing them to represent anything from money to identity.

Another foundational idea is tokenomics—the study of how tokens function within an ecosystem. Tokenomics includes supply limits, distribution schedules, utility, incentives, governance rights, and rewards. A strong tokenomic model can attract users, align stakeholders, and create sustainable long-term growth. Poor tokenomics can lead to rapid inflation, lack of demand, and a failing ecosystem. Understanding tokenomics helps users evaluate which projects have real potential and which are short-lived speculative ventures.

Staking is a key mechanism in modern blockchains. When users stake tokens, they lock them into a network to help secure the blockchain. In return, they earn rewards. Staking is passive income generated through participation rather than speculation. It turns users into active contributors in the decentralized economy. Many DeFi platforms also allow users to earn yield by providing liquidity, lending assets, or participating in automated market-making systems.

Tokens revolutionize global finance by removing friction. Traditional banks cannot move money instantly across borders without delays, fees, and approvals. Tokens move in seconds. They are programmable, meaning smart contracts can trigger payments automatically. They have no banking hours, no national boundaries, and no discrimination. This makes tokens one of the most inclusive financial technologies ever created.

In Web 3.0, tokens are not just investments—they are tools. They give users identity, access, power, rights, rewards, and ownership. They make decentralized applications possible. They fuel innovation across industries. Tokens turn the internet from a viewing platform into a participatory economy.

Understanding tokens is essential because they will shape the future of global commerce, entertainment, identity, governance, gaming, and work.

"The Token That Was More Than Money"

Javier had never given much thought to cryptocurrencies. He'd heard about Bitcoin on the news, watched people argue about Ethereum online, and seen NFTs trend on social media, but he always assumed it was just Internet hype. That changed one afternoon when he visited an art café owned by his friend Serena, a digital painter whose work had started gaining attention in Web 3.0 circles. When he walked in, he saw her installing a projection of colorful animated artwork that shimmered across the walls like living murals.

"What is all this?" Javier asked. Serena smiled. "It's my NFT gallery. Tonight's the opening." Javier blinked. "You're showing NFTs... in real life?" Serena nodded proudly. "It's more than a show. It's a marketplace, a membership, a community gathering. All powered by tokens." Javier laughed, thinking she was joking. She wasn't.

Serena walked him through the space. Each artwork was paired with a digital token displayed on a screen. "These aren't just files," she said. "Each NFT represents ownership, royalties, access, and identity." Javier watched as visitors connected their digital wallets to view hidden layers of the art that only collectors could unlock. Others scanned QR codes to join a token-gated Discord community. The café's back room was reserved for holders of a special governance token that allowed them to help plan future exhibits.

Javier felt his skepticism melting away. This wasn't hype—it was an ecosystem.

Later that evening, Serena surprised him with a small NFT as a gift—a shimmering digital feather with the words "Member #247." "This token gives you lifetime access to my workshops," she said. "Plus you get voting rights. You're officially part of the community now." Javier opened his wallet app, and there it was: a token that wasn't money, but meant something. Something personal.

When he went home that night, he kept staring at the feather. It wasn't just a picture. It was proof he belonged somewhere. It was access. It was identity. It was a key to a world he didn't yet understand. Over the next few days, Javier became curious. He started reading about tokens. He learned the difference between cryptocurrencies, governance tokens, utility tokens, and NFTs. He discovered that tokens powered metaverse worlds, games, decentralized apps, and global organizations with no CEOs.

One day he joined a virtual meeting for Serena's community. To his shock, people around the world were voting on proposals—event ideas, artist collaborations, even budget allocations. All executed by smart contracts. Javier realized the token in his wallet wasn't just an access pass. It was a voice. It was influence.

Soon he discovered staking and tried earning rewards by locking tokens into networks that needed validators. He learned how tokens secured blockchains, powered DeFi loans, and moved across borders instantly. He found himself helping newcomers understand what tokens were—not as speculative assets, but as tools that transformed the way humans cooperate digitally.

One afternoon, as he walked into Serena's café, he paused in front of a mural that now displayed his feather NFT in a rotating gallery of community members. A young artist approached him and said, "You're the reason I joined yesterday. Your explanation of tokens helped me understand everything."

In that moment, Javier realized the truth: the feather had changed his life. Not because of its monetary value, but because it represented something deeper—belonging, creativity, participation, and opportunity.

“It wasn’t just a token,” Javier thought. “It was my doorway.”

Chapter 6

Decentralized Finance (DeFi): The New Global Money System

Decentralized Finance—commonly called DeFi—is one of the most transformative innovations of Web 3.0. While traditional finance depends on banks, brokerage firms, credit institutions, and centralized authorities to manage transactions, lending, borrowing, trading, and savings, DeFi replaces all of that with smart contracts running on public blockchains. In DeFi, financial services function like machines—automatic, transparent, programmable, and global—without requiring trust in institutions. This creates a new financial system that is borderless, permissionless, and accessible to anyone with an internet connection. DeFi is not a future concept; it already handles billions of dollars in transactions every day.

To understand DeFi, you must begin with its core principles. First, DeFi removes intermediaries. Instead of banks approving a loan, smart contracts handle the process instantly. Instead of brokers taking fees for trades, decentralized exchanges allow users to swap assets directly. Instead of relying on centralized databases, DeFi platforms use blockchains to verify and record all transactions. This decentralized architecture makes the system more resilient, efficient, and fair. Second, DeFi is permissionless. Anyone, regardless of location, income level, credit score, or nationality, can participate. There are no application forms, no gatekeepers, and no micro-level approvals. Finally, DeFi is transparent. Every transaction, rule, and contract is visible on-chain for anyone to audit. This openness reduces corruption and creates trust at scale.

The foundation of DeFi is built using smart contracts, which automate traditional financial functions. These smart contracts run on blockchains like Ethereum, Solana, Avalanche, Polygon, and others. Because smart contracts execute exactly as programmed, users do not need to rely on companies or governments to honor agreements. Instead, they rely on code. This eliminates delays, unexpected fees, and subjective decision-making. For example, a DeFi lending platform like Aave or Compound allows users to supply tokens to a liquidity pool where borrowers can instantly borrow against collateral. Everything—interest rates, collateral requirements, liquidation thresholds—is governed by smart contracts. Users retain control of their funds at all times.

Decentralized exchanges (DEXs) are another core element of DeFi. Unlike traditional exchanges such as Coinbase or Binance that operate as centralized businesses, DEXs like Uniswap, SushiSwap, PancakeSwap, and Raydium allow users to trade tokens directly from their wallets. There is no need to create accounts, submit identification documents, or rely on third-party custodians. Trading occurs peer-to-peer through liquidity pools created by users. These pools allow traders to swap assets instantly and algorithmically, with prices determined by mathematical formulas rather than centralized order books. Liquidity providers earn fees for contributing assets, creating decentralized markets powered entirely by the community.

Liquidity pools are essential in the DeFi ecosystem. Users deposit pairs of tokens into a pool to enable trades between them. In return, they earn a portion of trading fees and sometimes additional token rewards. While liquidity provision can generate attractive returns, it comes with risks, such as impermanent loss—a temporary difference in value between providing liquidity and holding tokens separately. Understanding these risks is crucial for navigating DeFi safely. However, when used wisely, liquidity pools democratize market-making, allowing everyday people to participate in roles once reserved for financial institutions.

Staking is another major component of DeFi. Staking involves locking tokens into blockchain networks to help validate transactions or secure the protocol. In return, stakers earn rewards, much like earning interest in a savings account—but often with significantly higher yields. Staking aligns incentives between users and networks, encouraging long-term participation and stability. Networks like Ethereum, Solana, Cardano, Polkadot, Avalanche, and others rely on staking to function. Staking is also used by DeFi platforms to incentivize liquidity, governance participation, and protocol growth.

Another powerful area of DeFi is yield farming, a strategy where users move assets between platforms to earn rewards. Yield farmers seek the highest returns across liquidity pools, lending platforms, staking mechanisms, and incentive programs. Although yield farming can produce high gains, it requires experience and careful risk assessment. Because DeFi evolves rapidly, opportunities shift frequently. Successful yield farmers understand smart contract risk, token inflation, liquidity dynamics, and market behavior. They use DeFi to generate passive income in ways that traditional finance cannot match.

Collateralized borrowing is another transformative innovation in DeFi. Instead of banks deciding loan eligibility, DeFi allows anyone to borrow using digital assets as collateral. For example, a user can deposit ETH into a lending protocol and borrow stablecoins like USDC or DAI against it. This creates liquidity without needing to sell long-term assets. If the value of the collateral falls below a certain threshold, the smart contract automatically liquidates enough collateral to repay the loan. This system is fair, predictable, and efficient. There are no credit checks, income requirements, or approval processes. Everything is governed by algorithms and code.

Stablecoins are essential to the DeFi ecosystem. These tokens are pegged to stable assets such as the U.S. dollar, allowing users to move money quickly and avoid volatility. Popular stablecoins include USDC, USDT, DAI, and FRAX. Stablecoins serve as a bridge between traditional and decentralized finance. They allow users to earn interest, trade, pay, borrow, or store value without exposure to crypto market swings. Many stablecoins are backed by reserves, while others use decentralized mechanisms to maintain their peg.

Decentralized autonomous organizations (DAOs) also play a major role in governing DeFi platforms. Many DeFi protocols are owned and controlled by their communities through governance tokens. Token holders vote on fee structures, reward rates, upgrades, partnerships, and treasury spending. This creates a financial system that is not only decentralized technologically but also decentralized politically. Instead of regulators or executives making decisions, the users shape the future of DeFi.

Despite its benefits, DeFi also carries risks. Smart contracts can contain bugs or vulnerabilities if not properly audited. Some projects may inflate token rewards unsustainably. Market volatility can cause liquidation events. Scams and fraudulent projects exist and must be avoided through careful research. However, these risks do not negate the value of DeFi—they simply require awareness and responsible participation. The same is true for early internet technologies; innovation often arrives with growing pains.

At its core, DeFi democratizes finance. It gives people control over their money. It eliminates unnecessary intermediaries. It provides opportunities traditionally reserved for wealthy investors or institutions. DeFi opens the door to borderless financial freedom. It is the gateway to a world where people—not banks—control their economic destinies.

"The Night the Bank Closed and DeFi Didn't"

Riley never thought much about banks—until the night she desperately needed them. Her younger brother, Daniel, was traveling abroad when he called in a panic. His wallet had been stolen. His cards were gone. He needed money fast. Riley opened her banking app only to find that her transfer limit had been reduced without warning. When she called customer service, the automated system told her she would need to verify her identity during business hours. Business hours.

Daniel didn't have until morning. He didn't have food or a place to stay.

Her frustration turned to anger. She had money. She wanted to help. But one institution stood between her and the person she loved. As she sat there helpless, she remembered a conversation she had brushed aside weeks earlier. Her coworker Zane had excitedly told her about DeFi—how money could move instantly, anytime, anywhere. She had laughed then. She wasn't laughing now.

Desperate, she messaged Zane: "Is that crypto thing still something I can learn tonight?" Within minutes, he arrived at her apartment, laptop in hand. "Okay," he said, "sit next to me. It's time you saw what money looks like without banks." He helped her set up a digital wallet, buy stablecoins, and connect to a DeFi platform. Riley's hands shook as she clicked each button, praying she wasn't making a mistake. Zane reassured her. "This is easier than you think. And faster than anything you've ever used."

He showed her a decentralized money transfer tool powered entirely by smart contracts. "Watch this," he said, guiding her through the process. She entered Daniel's wallet address, typed the amount, and pressed send. A single second later, a notification pinged on Daniel's phone. The money had arrived instantly. No limits. No approvals. No business hours. Riley gasped, tears forming in her eyes. “Why didn’t I know about this?” she whispered. Zane smiled gently. “Because the old system doesn’t want you to.” The next day, Riley became obsessed with understanding how DeFi worked. She learned about liquidity pools, where ordinary people acted as the market makers. She discovered staking, where anyone could earn rewards by supporting blockchain networks. She watched tutorials explaining decentralized exchanges, where users traded without giving up custody of their funds. She joined online spaces filled with people from all over the world—students, retirees, bankers-turned-believers—sharing insights and opportunities.

One story struck her deeply: a farmer in Asia who used DeFi loans to expand his land after local banks rejected him. Another was a single mother who earned passive income by contributing to liquidity pools. Riley began to realize DeFi wasn’t about getting rich—it was about fairness. It gave power to people who had been ignored or excluded for decades. It offered a way to participate in the global economy without privilege or permission.

Weeks passed, and Riley’s understanding grew. One evening, she invited a few friends over for dinner. They exchanged the usual small talk until one asked about her sudden interest in crypto. Riley didn't talk about profits or speculation. Instead, she told them about Daniel. About the fear she felt that night. About the system that failed her. And about the moment DeFi didn't. Her friends were captivated. "It sounds like magic," one said. Riley shook her head. "Not magic. Just freedom." She showed them how a liquidity pool worked, pouring candies into two bowls to mimic token pairs. She illustrated staking with slips of paper representing validators. She demonstrated instant transfers live, sending a small amount to their phones. By the end of the night, they were staring at her like she had discovered fire.

But the moment she truly understood DeFi's power came a month later. Daniel called again—not in distress this time, but with excitement. "I've been learning too," he said. "I started staking. And lending. And..." Riley's smile widened as he explained everything he had done with small amounts of money. He wasn't being reckless—he was participating. He was learning. He was growing.

As she hung up, Riley walked to her window and stared at the city lights. Millions of people below her were living inside a financial system they didn't understand, controlled by institutions they didn't choose. But above that system—quietly, globally—was DeFi, always awake, always open, always fair.

"Someday," she whispered, "everyone will know."

And she knew she would help them learn.

Chapter 7

DAOs (Decentralized Autonomous Organizations): The Future of Communities, Companies & Collaboration

DAOs—Decentralized Autonomous Organizations—represent one of the most radical evolutions of Web 3.0. A DAO is an online community, business, or organization that operates through blockchain-based smart contracts rather than traditional corporate structures. Instead of CEOs, managers, or executives making the decisions, members vote collectively using governance tokens. Instead of centralized bank accounts, DAOs use decentralized treasuries controlled by smart contracts. Instead of private boardrooms, DAOs hold public discussions where anyone can propose ideas. This new form of organization redefines how humans collaborate, invest, build, create, and govern in the digital age.

To understand DAOs clearly, imagine a cooperative that runs entirely online, without a physical office, without a hierarchical structure, and without people acting as gatekeepers. The rules of the organization are encoded transparently in smart contracts. Funding decisions, membership guidelines, project distributions, and treasury transactions are all recorded on the blockchain. This transparency eliminates corruption, secrecy, and fraud. It ensures that decisions are made based on community choice rather than private influence. Every action is traceable and auditable by anyone.

At the most basic level, a DAO consists of three elements: its community (the members), its treasury (shared funds), and its governance mechanism (usually token-based voting). Members hold governance tokens, which grant them voting rights. The more tokens someone holds, the more influence they have—but this influence is limited by smart contracts to prevent manipulation and abuse. When someone wants to change something—allocate funds, hire contributors, support a project, or upgrade the protocol—they submit a proposal. Token holders then vote, and if the proposal meets the required threshold, the smart contract automatically executes the decision.

DAOs can be formed for countless purposes. Investment DAOs pool funds to invest in startups, digital assets, or metaverse property. Creator DAOs help artists collaborate, support each other, and collectively own intellectual property. Social DAOs form communities around shared interests, events, or cultural movements. Protocol DAOs govern major DeFi platforms, deciding fees, rewards, upgrades, and long-term strategy. Collector DAOs focus on acquiring NFTs or digital art. Service DAOs operate like decentralized agencies, offering development, design, marketing, or operational services to other Web 3.0 projects. This diversity makes DAOs a flexible and powerful model for global collaboration.

One of the most powerful aspects of DAOs is decentralized governance. Traditional organizations rely on executives who often make decisions behind closed doors, influenced by personal agendas or corporate politics. DAOs eliminate this dynamic. Anyone can submit proposals. Anyone can vote. Anyone can track how funds are spent. This democratizes organizational power and unlocks creativity from people who would otherwise remain unheard. A college student in Brazil can propose a partnership. A developer in India can vote on protocol upgrades. A designer in Kenya can join a working group. Geography, status, and age become irrelevant.

DAOs also reinvent how work is performed. Instead of full-time employees with fixed roles, DAOs utilize contributors—individuals who complete tasks, submit deliverables, or join short-term teams to accomplish goals. Contributors earn tokens or stablecoins as compensation. This model is flexible, global, and merit-based. People can work for multiple DAOs at once. They can build a resume of on-chain activity. Their value is measured by contributions, not credentials. This represents the beginning of "on-chain careers," where someone's reputation is proven through blockchain transactions and verified history rather than paper resumes.

Treasury management is another groundbreaking shift introduced by DAOs. Instead of a centralized account controlled by a small team, DAOs store funds in multi-signature wallets or smart contract treasuries that require community approval for spending. This creates financial transparency beyond anything seen in traditional institutions. Anyone can inspect the treasury balance, track expenses, or audit financial decisions. This level of accountability reduces fraud, misuse, and corruption dramatically. Funds are deployed based on community decisions, not executive preferences.

DAOs also utilize tokens to incentivize alignment. Members who participate actively—by voting, contributing, organizing, or completing tasks—often earn additional governance tokens. This means the DAO rewards people who take part in its growth. Contributors become stakeholders, and stakeholders become contributors. This alignment strengthens community loyalty and long-term commitment. It creates shared ownership and collective responsibility.

But DAOs are not without challenges. Decentralized decision-making can be slow, especially when large groups are involved. Poorly designed voting structures can lead to low participation, concentration of power, or governance attacks by malicious actors. Smart contract vulnerabilities can expose treasuries to risk if not properly audited. Legal recognition remains an evolving landscape; some jurisdictions now recognize DAOs as legal entities, while others do not. Despite these challenges, DAOs continue to grow rapidly because they offer something traditional institutions cannot—global, transparent, community-owned organizations built for the digital age.

The true power of DAOs lies in their ability to coordinate at scale. Thousands of people across different countries, cultures, and time zones can collaborate effectively without centralized leadership. DAOs enable crowdfunding, community ownership, collective creativity, and decentralized governance to operate seamlessly. They redefine what a company is, what a community is, and how the world organizes itself.

In Web 3.0, DAOs are not just organizations—they are movements. They are the new digital nations, the new corporations, the new cooperatives, the new studios, and the new communities that will shape culture, technology, finance, and the metaverse for decades to come.

"The DAO That Had No Leader"

Naomi had spent most of her adult life working inside big corporations. She knew the routine: morning meetings, layers of managers, endless email chains, and decisions made by people who rarely understood the ground-level work. She wanted something different–something meaningful, something empowering—but every company she joined felt the same. That changed the day her friend, Oliver, invited her to a virtual event titled: *"How to Work for an Organization With No Boss."* She joined out of curiosity, not expecting much. By the end of the call, her entire understanding of work had changed.

The event was hosted by a group called Horizon Guild, a global DAO dedicated to supporting new Web 3.0 builders. The host, a soft-spoken woman named Samira, began by asking, "Who here is tired of hierarchies?" Dozens of people raised their hands. Naomi felt her own rising.

Samira explained that Horizon Guild had no CEO, no headquarters, and no management ladder. "Our community proposes ideas, votes, executes tasks, and pays contributors–automatically," she said. "Everything is on-chain. Everything is transparent. Everyone has a voice." Naomi leaned forward, skeptical but intrigued. How could an organization with no leaders function? How could it avoid chaos?

To demonstrate, Samira opened the DAO dashboard. Naomi watched as proposals scrolled by: funding a new developer, sponsoring an event, designing brand content, translating tutorials. Each proposal had votes attached—green for yes, red for no. Every participant had a governance token. The more someone contributed, the more tokens they earned, increasing their influence. It was a democracy that actually worked.

Curiosity pulled Naomi deeper. She joined the DAO's forum. She introduced herself. Within minutes, people from around the world welcomed her—artists from Nigeria, coders from Italy, entrepreneurs from Canada, students from Singapore. They spoke like equals. No one asked for her credentials. No one cared about her job title. They cared about what she could do.

The next day, she noticed a proposal asking for volunteers to create onboarding guides for new members. Without overthinking it, she submitted a short draft. Within hours, members upvoted her contribution and tipped her a small amount of governance tokens. She hadn't asked for payment. She hadn't negotiated a rate. She was simply rewarded because the DAO valued her work.

That moment felt magical.

Over the next two weeks, Naomi participated in more tasks. She wrote documentation, helped organize a community workshop, and joined a small working group improving member engagement. There were no bosses assigning tasks. People volunteered for whatever aligned with their skills and interests. Everyone took ownership. Everyone contributed because they cared—because they were part of something bigger.

But the moment that changed everything came during a major vote. The DAO needed to decide how to allocate funds from a newly secured grant. Three proposals were on the table: fund a mentorship program, support a metaverse build, or launch a global hackathon. Naomi read each proposal carefully. She researched the authors. She analyzed the impact. And then, for the first time in her life, she voted on an organizational decision where her vote held equal weight to everyone else.

It felt empowering. It felt meaningful. It felt right.

When the results came in, the mentorship program won. Seconds later, the DAO's smart contract automatically moved funds from the treasury to a dedicated wallet. No approvals. No bureaucracy. No managers. Just action. Naomi felt goosebumps. The organization did in seconds what her previous employers took weeks or months to accomplish.

Inspired, she decided to propose her own initiative—a multilingual content library to help global newcomers understand Web 3.0. She expected a handful of votes. Instead, her proposal exploded with support. Members added ideas, offered help, and committed resources. When the vote passed, the smart contract initiated the project instantly. And Naomi, once a quiet corporate employee, became the coordinator of a global initiative supported by hundreds of people.

Months passed, and Naomi's life transformed. She no longer felt trapped in meetings or buried under bureaucracy. She worked with people who respected her. She earned tokens for contributions she loved making. She participated in decisions that mattered. She saw real impact. And she realized she had finally found what she had always been searching for: a place where she belonged, where her voice mattered, and where work felt like collaboration rather than control.

One evening, while reviewing her dashboard, she paused and smiled. There were no bosses. No managers. No executives. And yet, the DAO ran more smoothly than any organization she had ever been part of. It operated on trust, transparency, and shared ownership.

"The DAO has no leader," she whispered to herself, "because we are all the leaders."

And for the first time in her career, she felt truly free.

Chapter 8

Web 3.0 Identity: Owning Your Digital Self (Wallets, ENS, SBTs & On-Chain Reputation)

Identity is one of the most important—and most misunderstood—components of Web 3.0. In Web 2.0, your identity is scattered across centralized platforms such as Google, Facebook, Instagram, LinkedIn, and dozens of websites that store your personal data, login credentials, behavioral patterns, and private information. These companies own your digital presence and monetize it without your permission. If any of them suspend your account, change their rules, or experience a data breach, your online identity becomes compromised. Web 3.0 transforms this paradigm by introducing decentralized identity—an identity you own, control, secure, transfer, and use without relying on corporations or governments. In Web 3.0, your identity becomes portable, self-sovereign, and verifiable anywhere in the digital world.

The foundation of Web 3.0 identity is the digital wallet. Unlike Web 2.0 accounts that are tied to emails and passwords stored on company servers, a Web 3.0 wallet is permissionless, pseudonymous, and entirely under your control. Your wallet address represents your digital identity across decentralized applications. When you sign into a dApp, the connection is cryptographic—not dependent on personal data. You share only what you choose to share. Your wallet becomes your gateway to assets, memberships, credentials, collectibles, reputation, and digital interactions. It is the digital equivalent of your passport, bank account, keys, and identity card—all combined in one sovereign tool.

But Web 3.0 identity extends far beyond wallet addresses. The Ethereum Name Service (ENS) introduces human-readable identities such as "yourname.eth," replacing long, complex wallet addresses with simple Web 3.0 usernames. An ENS name can function like a social handle, business card, website, email, or universal login. Because ENS names are NFTs, you truly own them. No company can take them away, censor them, or dictate how you use them. They become digital property that defines your presence across the decentralized internet. ENS is one of many emerging decentralized naming systems, each expanding the possibilities for digital identity.

Soulbound tokens (SBTs) represent another revolutionary step. Unlike NFTs or cryptocurrencies, SBTs cannot be transferred. They are permanently bound to your wallet, representing achievements, membership, certifications, credentials, academic records, loyalty tiers, medical history, game experience, or proof of participation. In traditional systems, these credentials are stored in institutions' databases; in Web 3.0, they live in your wallet, verifiable by anyone and impossible to forge. SBTs create a portable, tamper-proof identity layer that travels with you across platforms, unlocking social, educational, professional, and financial opportunities.

On-chain reputation is rapidly becoming one of the most powerful elements of decentralized identity. In Web 2.0, reputation is centralized and platform-specific—your Uber rating does not follow you to Airbnb, and your LinkedIn recommendations do not influence your YouTube performance. In Web 3.0, reputation is unified and cross-platform. Every on-chain action—votes, contributions, DAO participation, NFT mints, completed tasks, staking history, lending activity, governance involvement—creates a verifiable track record. Your wallet becomes your résumé. Your contribution history becomes your proof of skill. Your on-chain footprint becomes your professional reputation. This creates a transparent, global merit-based system where opportunities flow to those with verifiable contributions rather than personal connections or corporate bias.

Decentralized identity also enhances privacy. Web 3.0 does not require users to reveal their legal names, addresses, or personal details to participate. Instead, identity is built through cryptographic proofs. Zero-knowledge proofs (ZKPs) represent a major breakthrough in this area. ZKPs allow users to verify information—such as being over 18, having sufficient funds, completing tasks, or possessing a credential—without disclosing any private data. This eliminates the need to overshare personal information, reducing the risk of surveillance, data leaks, hacking, and exploitation. The power dynamic shifts dramatically: platforms no longer extract identity information—you selectively provide cryptographic proofs instead.

Another dimension of decentralized identity is token-gated access. In Web 3.0, access to communities, metaverse worlds, events, software tools, guilds, and private experiences can be granted based on tokens held in your wallet. This transforms identity into a programmable object. Instead of logging into a platform with a username and password, your wallet automatically verifies whether you qualify. Identity becomes dynamic, flexible, and completely user-owned. Token-gated systems eliminate fake accounts, bots, and identity fraud because access depends on verifiable blockchain ownership rather than easily manipulated personal data.

Web 3.0 identity is also redefining professional credentials. On-chain credentials issued through SBTs, NFTs, or verifiable reputation systems can prove skills, project contributions, and work history without relying on centralized LinkedIn profiles or resumes. Employers, DAOs, clients, and collaborators can instantly validate your expertise by checking your wallet's on-chain activity. This creates a transparent, global talent marketplace where skill and contribution outweigh formal titles or degrees. For freelancers and global workers, on-chain identity unlocks opportunities that were previously limited by geography or institutional bias.

Digital identity in Web 3.0 is not just technological—it's social. Communities form around wallet-based membership, shared token ownership, and decentralized governance. These communities are borderless and inclusive, enabling people from all cultures and backgrounds to collaborate without needing formal permission. Social reputation becomes an asset. Participation earns visibility. Contribution earns respect. Identity becomes fluid, evolving in real time based on your interactions across the decentralized ecosystem.

There are challenges, of course. Linking identities across chains, protecting privacy, preventing wallet theft, designing ethical reputation metrics, and maintaining decentralized governance are ongoing challenges. But the momentum is undeniable. Web 3.0 identity is already reshaping how people interact online. It empowers individuals to own their data, define their presence, protect their privacy, and build a transparent reputation that cannot be erased or manipulated by corporations.

In Web 3.0, you are no longer a product. You are the owner—of your identity, your data, your reputation, and your digital life.

"YourName.eth"

Kira never liked the feeling of being controlled online. Every time she logged into a social platform, she whispered a small prayer that her password would work and her account wouldn't be locked. She'd been banned once—by mistake—and the experience traumatized her. Years of posts, photos, messages, and memories vanished instantly, and no customer support agent ever responded. That was the moment she realized she didn't own anything online. She was a guest in someone else's house, allowed to stay only as long as the algorithm smiled on her.

Everything changed the day she attended a workshop titled *"Own Your Digital Self."* She expected another long lecture about passwords and cybersecurity. Instead, she encountered something far more powerful—Web 3.0 identity.

The host, a soft-spoken developer named Lina, began by asking the audience a simple question: "Who here truly owns their online identity?" Silence filled the room. Kira felt a pang of discomfort. Lina continued, "In Web 2.0, your identity can be deleted, altered, or sold without your consent. In Web 3.0, your identity belongs only to you."

As Lina explained decentralized identity, wallets, ENS names, and soulbound tokens, Kira felt something she hadn't felt in years: hope. The idea that her identity could be portable, permanent, and invulnerable to corporate rules thrilled her. After the workshop, she rushed home and created her first Web 3.0 wallet. It felt like opening a blank passport—full of potential.

Then she bought her ENS name: **KiraNova.eth**.

The moment she confirmed the transaction and saw her new name appear in her wallet, something inside her shifted. This wasn't a username. It wasn't rented or borrowed. It was hers—forever. No one could take it away. She owned her digital identity for the first time in her life.

Over the next weeks, Kira began exploring what her new identity could do. She connected her ENS name to a decentralized profile, linking her NFTs, contributions, and credentials. She claimed soulbound tokens from events she attended, courses she completed, and DAOs she contributed to. Her identity evolved organically, shaped by her actions rather than platform rules. One day, she applied to join a Web 3.0 writing collective. Instead of uploading a résumé, she simply shared her wallet address. The collective reviewed her on-chain activity—her past contributions, projects, reputation, and credentials. "Your work speaks for itself," the reviewer told her. "Your on-chain identity is stronger than a résumé." Kira felt a rush of pride. She hadn't realized how powerful her digital footprint had become.

Soon she discovered token-gated communities where holding specific NFTs granted access. For the first time, she entered spaces free of bots, trolls, or spam—because every member had verifiable ownership. These communities felt genuine. Kind. Human. She made friends in Lisbon, Singapore, Buenos Aires, and Nairobi—people who treated her not as a profile picture but as a respected contributor.

But the moment that changed her life came when she attended her first metaverse conference. As she connected her wallet, her avatar instantly transformed into a custom skin linked to one of her NFTs. Her name hovered above her: **KiraNova.eth**. People approached her, recognizing her contributions from the writing collective, the DAO discussions, and the soulbound tokens she carried. Her identity wasn't just a name—it was a reputation, a history, and a badge of trust.

During one panel, a speaker announced a new global initiative to create multilingual educational content. Volunteers were welcome. Kira felt a spark. She raised her hand. "I can help write," she said. The moderator smiled. "Wallet address?" Kira gave her ENS name. In minutes, she was added as a contributor and received a soulbound token marking her participation.

When she returned home that evening, she opened her wallet and stared at her growing collection of achievements. Not badges in a game or likes on a post—but verifiable proof of who she was becoming. Her identity was no longer fragile. No longer dependent on corporate approval. No longer vulnerable to algorithms.

Her identity was hers—owned, protected, evolving, and unbreakable.

She whispered softly, "This... is me."

And for the first time in her life, she believed it.

Chapter 9

Web 3.0 Security: Protecting Your Wallet, Assets, Identity, and Reputation

Security is one of the most essential topics in Web 3.0. While blockchain technology itself is incredibly secure—far more secure than traditional centralized databases—the responsibility for protecting your assets and identity shifts heavily onto the user. This is both empowering and intimidating. In Web 2.0, platforms store your data, recover your passwords, and maintain control over your accounts. In Web 3.0, you are in full control, which means you must understand best practices to stay safe. The good news is that once you understand how Web 3.0 security works, protecting your assets becomes simple, powerful, and far more reliable than traditional systems. Security is not about fear—it is about knowledge, ownership, and empowerment.

The most important security principle in Web 3.0 is custodianship. In decentralized systems, you are the custodian of your private keys, seed phrase, and digital identity. Your seed phrase is the master key to your wallet. Whoever has it controls everything you own. This means it must never be stored digitally, and never shared with anyone—not friends, not family, not customer support, not websites, not screenshots, and not cloud backups. The safest storage method is offline, ideally written on paper or engraved in metal, stored in a safe place. Losing your seed phrase means permanently losing access to your assets. Sharing it means giving control to someone else. This responsibility is what makes Web 3.0 powerful—because only you hold the keys.

The second foundational principle is understanding how wallet connections and permissions work. When you connect your wallet to a decentralized application, you grant that application a certain level of permission to interact with your assets. Most of the time, these permissions are harmless and temporary, but malicious platforms can request unlimited spending approvals, tricking users into signing transactions that drain their funds. To avoid this, you should always review transaction requests carefully and only connect your wallet to reputable platforms. Many users also periodically revoke permissions using tools that scan for approved smart contracts. This adds another layer of protection.

Smart contract risks are another consideration. While major DeFi platforms, NFT marketplaces, and DAOs undergo extensive audits to ensure contract safety, smaller or newer projects may contain vulnerabilities. Hackers often exploit poorly written smart contracts rather than breaking blockchains themselves. This is why research is critical. Before interacting with an unfamiliar contract, check whether the project has audits, active development, and a credible team. Use only trusted marketplaces and verified contract addresses. Smart contracts are powerful but must be interacted with intelligently.

Another principle of Web 3.0 security is recognizing social engineering attacks. Scammers often succeed not by hacking technology but by manipulating people. This includes fake airdrops, phishing links, fraudulent customer support accounts, urgent messages claiming your wallet is compromised, or fake mint events for popular NFT drops. These scams rely on panic, urgency, and deception. The rule in Web 3.0 is simple: official teams will never ask for your private key or seed phrase, and you should never click unknown links or connect your wallet to random websites. If something feels rushed or too good to be true, it usually is.

Hardware wallets represent the highest level of protection for your assets. These devices store your private keys offline, making them immune to most digital attacks. Even if your computer is compromised, your assets remain safe as long as your hardware wallet is secure. Serious users, long-term holders, investors, and builders treat hardware wallets as essential tools. They provide peace of mind and significantly reduce the risk of hacks and phishing attacks. Hardware wallets are often used for long-term or high-value storage, while browser or mobile wallets are used for daily interactions.

Security also extends to your digital identity. Because your reputation and credentials live on-chain, protecting your wallet protects your identity as well. This includes safeguarding your ENS name, soulbound tokens, DAO memberships, and on-chain achievements. Losing access to your wallet does not only mean losing tokens—it means losing your digital identity and reputation. This is why many users separate their long-term identity wallet from their daily-use wallet. Your identity wallet can remain offline or secured with maximum protection, while your daily wallet interacts with dApps and platforms.

Decentralized security also involves understanding the role of zero-knowledge proofs (ZKPs), multisig wallets, and social recovery. Zero-knowledge-proof systems allow users to verify their identity or eligibility without exposing personal information. Multisig wallets require multiple approvals to unlock funds, providing added protection for DAOs, treasuries, and high-value holdings. Social recovery methods allow users to appoint trusted individuals or devices to help restore access if a wallet is compromised—without revealing private keys. These innovations give users flexibility while maintaining decentralization. Another important security concept is understanding network risks. Different blockchains operate with different levels of security, validator strength, decentralization, and attack resistance. Large blockchains like Ethereum and Bitcoin are extremely secure due to their size and distribution. Smaller or newer chains may be more vulnerable to attacks. When interacting with a new blockchain, research its security model, validator set, and track record. Understanding network security helps you choose where to store assets and where to transact safely.

Finally, Web 3.0 security includes learning from community culture. Every major crypto community publishes safety guides, scam alerts, verified contract addresses, and trusted resources. There are channels dedicated to reporting vulnerabilities, tracking exploits, and educating users. The Web 3.0 community takes security seriously because it understands the stakes. Participating in these communities not only increases your knowledge but also protects you from common mistakes.

In Web 3.0, security is not fear—it is empowerment. Traditional systems rely on institutions to protect your identity, assets, and information, yet those institutions frequently fail. Web 3.0 gives you the tools to protect yourself. Once you understand how to secure your wallet, identify risks, use hardware devices, verify smart contracts, and control your identity, your digital life becomes safer, more private, more independent, and more sovereign than ever before. Security is freedom.

"The Wallet That Almost Got Away"

Landon considered himself tech-savvy. He worked in IT, fixed computers for fun, and learned new software faster than most people learned to use their phones. But Web 3.0 humbled him in a way he didn't expect. His journey into decentralized security began the night he almost lost everything.

It happened after he joined an online NFT community. The group was friendly, energetic, and full of people excited about a future drop. One evening, while chatting in their Discord server, a message appeared from what looked like one of the moderators: **"Emergency update! Connect your wallet here or you may lose your whitelist spot."** Landon clicked the link without thinking—after all, he trusted the community.

The moment he connected his wallet, something felt wrong. The site looked off—sloppy, rushed, unpolished. His stomach twisted. He quickly opened his wallet activity log and saw a pending transaction that allowed unlimited spending permissions. His heart stopped. If he had signed it, the scammers would have drained everything he owned. His NFTs, tokens, and even his ENS name—gone.

Hands shaking, he rejected the transaction. Then he closed the tab, disconnected his wallet, and sat back, breathing hard. He had nearly lost years of savings and an identity he had spent months building. All because of one rushed click.

The next day, Landon joined a Web 3.0 security workshop in desperation. The host, an older man named Felix, had a calm voice and eyes full of experience. "Many of us learn the hard way," Felix began. "But once you understand Web 3.0 security, you'll never make the same mistake again." Landon listened carefully, absorbing every word. Felix explained wallet permissions, transaction signatures, phishing links, malicious contracts, and the importance of hardware wallets.

Felix said something that stuck with Landon forever: "Web 2.0 users depend on companies to save them. Web 3.0 users save themselves." Those words rewired something in Landon's mind.

He bought a hardware wallet that same night. Setting it up felt strangely empowering—like installing a vault door on his digital life. He wrote down his seed phrase carefully, storing copies in two separate places. For the first time, he truly understood what it meant to *own* something online.

But the story didn't end there. A week later, he noticed a new member in the NFT community asking for help. She was young, nervous, and clearly overwhelmed. Someone had sent her a suspicious link, and she wasn't sure if she should click it. Landon stepped in quickly, explaining what to look for, how to verify safety, and how to avoid mistakes he had nearly made himself. She thanked him with genuine relief, and he realized he had just prevented someone else from experiencing the fear he had felt.

Over the following months, Landon became the unofficial security mentor of the group. He helped newcomers set up wallets, taught them how to read transaction details, explained smart contract risks, and guided them toward safe practices. He created simple checklists, recorded short tutorials, and shared scam alerts. People from all over the world messaged him privately for advice. He became the person he wished he had met earlier.

His proudest moment came when a teenager from Brazil messaged him saying, "You saved my entire wallet today. Thank you." Landon felt a warmth in his chest. Web 3.0 wasn't just about assets—it was about people helping each other learn to protect themselves.

One night, as he sat at his desk reviewing new security tools, he looked at his hardware wallet resting beside him. A small device, but with immense significance. It represented independence, sovereignty, and lessons learned the hard way. He smiled to himself.

He had almost lost everything. But instead, he had gained wisdom—and a mission.

“This time,” he whispered, “the wallet didn’t get away.”

And it never would again.

Chapter 10

The Future of Web 3.0: Predictions, Opportunities, and What Comes Next

The future of Web 3.0 is far more expansive than cryptocurrencies, NFTs, or decentralized applications. It represents a foundational shift in how humans interact, work, learn, build, and organize value on a global scale. As we transition from centralized digital ecosystems into decentralized, user-owned digital economies, we will witness rapid transformations across finance, identity, entertainment, governance, real estate, education, healthcare, and global collaboration. Understanding the direction of Web 3.0 is essential not only for participation but for leadership in this new era.

The first major evolution of Web 3.0 is mass adoption of blockchain-backed ownership across every digital platform. Currently, most digital items—game skins, in-app purchases, online assets—are not owned by users. Companies lock them behind restrictive ecosystems. Web 3.0 breaks these walls by enabling universal digital ownership via tokens. In coming years, everything from social media profiles to loyalty points, game items, educational certifications, music royalties, event tickets, digital clothing, and metaverse assets will transition into blockchain-based formats. This shift will unlock trillions of dollars in digital property that users truly own, trade, transfer, or monetize without intermediaries. Digital ownership will become as normal as physical ownership is today.

The next major evolution will occur in social platforms. Web 2.0 social media extracts value from users and controls their data, privacy, and monetization. Web 3.0 social platforms—powered by decentralized identity, portable social graphs, and tokenized incentives—return control and earnings to creators. Users will own their audience relationships. Platforms will no longer dictate reach, algorithms, or monetization rates. Instead, users will interact through wallet-based identities, social tokens, reputation layers, and tokenized content economies. Creators will earn royalties every time their content is shared, remixed, or referenced—perpetually. Fans will own pieces of creator ecosystems, forming deeper community bonds. Social media will transform into value-sharing networks where creators and users prosper together.

Another powerful evolution will happen in the workplace. Web 3.0 introduces the concept of the "wallet-to-work economy," where people earn income directly through smart contracts based on completed tasks, contributions, or on-chain credentials. Instead of résumés, job history will be verifiable on-chain. Instead of formal employment agreements, people will receive assignments through DAOs, decentralized teams, and tokenized marketplaces. Professionals will work across multiple DAOs simultaneously, building a diversified career portfolio. Compensation will be instant, global, and permissionless. Work will become fluid, flexible, and merit-based. Geographic limitations will disappear. A teenager in India could earn the same opportunities as an engineer in New York purely through on-chain contribution.

Another breakthrough area of Web 3.0 will be decentralized governance. As DAOs mature, they will influence not only digital platforms but real-world organizations, non-profits, investment funds, creative studios, political movements, scientific communities, and public infrastructure projects. Thousands of people will collaborate globally without needing traditional leadership structures. Important decisions—from funding scientific research to managing community resources—will be executed through transparent voting and smart contract automation. This decentralized governance model will challenge existing institutions and reshape how societies organize themselves. It will create digital nations, tokenized voting systems, and new models of collective ownership.

The metaverse will also evolve as an integral layer of Web 3.0. Instead of centralized metaverse worlds owned by corporations, decentralized metaverse platforms will flourish—where users own land, assets, experiences, and identity. Cross-platform avatars will allow seamless movement between virtual worlds. Tokenized assets will be interoperable across ecosystems. Virtual jobs, education, entertainment, and commerce will become mainstream. Companies will operate virtual storefronts, schools will teach in immersive environments, and businesses will host decentralized events for global audiences. As augmented reality and virtual reality advance, the boundary between physical and digital experiences will fade.

Interoperability will be a defining characteristic of Web 3.0's future. Today, digital ecosystems are isolated. But tomorrow, identity, assets, reputation, and apps will function across blockchains and platforms. Users will not notice whether they are interacting on Ethereum, Solana, Polygon, Avalanche, Arbitrum, or future chains. Bridges, rollups, L2 scaling technologies, and new consensus models will make blockchain interactions faster, cheaper, and more seamless. Web 3.0 will become invisible—the technology powering everything behind the scenes just like the internet today.

Artificial intelligence will merge with Web 3.0 in profound ways. AI agents will operate DAOs, optimize strategies, assist with governance, evaluate proposals, manage token economics, and support decision-making. Users will employ AI-powered on-chain assistants that manage portfolios, find opportunities, automate tasks, create content, verify contracts, and protect assets. AI and Web 3.0 together will create autonomous digital economies capable of self-organization and continuous adaptation.

One of the most important innovations still to come is decentralized identity becoming universal. Governments, schools, corporations, medical institutions, and global service providers will adopt blockchain-based identity standards. Individuals will own portable, cryptographically verified identities containing credentials, medical records, educational transcripts, employment history, and financial profiles. This will eliminate fraud, reduce administrative costs, and empower individuals to control who can access their data. Identity will become secure, global, and user-owned.

Challenges will remain—scalability, user experience, regulation, privacy, safety, and education. But as tools improve and adoption spreads, Web 3.0 will transition from niche to universal. Children born today will grow up in a world where wallets are normal, tokens are standard, DAOs are employers, and decentralized identity is the default.

Web 3.0 is not just a technological revolution—it is a philosophical one. It redefines ownership. It restructures power. It distributes value. It shifts control from institutions to individuals. This is the future of the internet. This is the future of global collaboration. This is the future of digital life. And everyone alive today is early.

"The World They Dreamed Of"

Marina sat on the balcony of her high-rise apartment, watching the lights of the city shimmer like stars scattered across earth. She was 22, finishing her final year of university, but none of her professors had prepared her for the world she was living in now. Everything was changing—faster than anyone expected. And for the first time, Marina felt she was not just witnessing history, but becoming part of it.

Her journey began two years earlier when she stumbled upon a hackathon hosted by a DAO focused on building public education tools in Web 3.0. She joined as an observer, shy and unsure, but quickly found herself mesmerized. People from around the world—developers, designers, educators, teenagers, retirees—were collaborating in real time, contributing ideas, voting on proposals, launching experiments, and earning rewards. There were no bosses. No geographical barriers. No permission needed. It felt like the internet when it first began—alive, hopeful, free.

Marina submitted a small idea: a tool that helped students verify academic credentials using soulbound tokens. She expected it to be ignored. Instead, it became one of the winning proposals. The DAO funded her project instantly through a smart contract. It was the first time she felt her ideas mattered. The first time she saw what decentralized collaboration could truly achieve.

Months passed, and her small tool evolved into a global initiative. Universities began testing it. Students in developing countries used it to prove their qualifications when applying for jobs abroad. Employers used the tool to validate credentials instantly without paperwork or bureaucracy. Marina watched as her idea helped thousands of people—and she didn't need a corporation, investors, or government approval. She needed only a wallet, a DAO, and a willingness to build.

As Web 3.0 grew, Marina witnessed countless innovations unfold. A musician in Seoul created a tokenized album that paid royalties to fans. A teacher in Brazil launched a DAO for local education, funded entirely by micro-donations. A small town in Kenya used decentralized governance to manage community water resources transparently. Students from four continents took virtual classes together inside a metaverse school. Identity became portable. Work became global. Ownership became universal. But the moment Marina truly understood the future came during a world summit hosted inside a decentralized metaverse. Leaders from DAOs, companies, universities, governments, and communities gathered—not in a physical building but in a vast virtual amphitheater floating among digital clouds. Marina attended as a contributor, not an outsider. She watched as people debated protocols for cross-chain identity, the ethics of AI-governed treasuries, and the role of decentralized social networks in elections.

During one discussion, a teenage girl from Nigeria spoke about using DAOs to fund solar panels for her village. The girl said, "We didn't wait for permission anymore. We didn't wait for governments to help us. We built our solution with the world." Marina felt tears gather in her eyes. That sentence captured everything she believed in.

Later that night, Marina wandered through a virtual forest simulation built by environmental researchers. She watched as a scientist demonstrated how on-chain data and AI could track global ecosystems in real time. She realized the future wasn't a prediction—it was happening right now, unfolding in front of her.

When the summit ended, Marina teleported back to her virtual office and stared out at a digital sunset. Her avatar glowed softly beneath a sky painted with shifting colors. She whispered, "The world is changing, and we get to build it." A message appeared on her screen—a new proposal asking for collaboration on a global education DAO. They wanted her input. They wanted her voice. They wanted her vision.

She accepted instantly.

Back on her physical balcony, the real city lights shimmered like a mirror of the metaverse she had just left. The future was no longer something distant or theoretical. It was tangible. It was alive. It was hers to shape.

And as she leaned forward, feeling the warm breeze brush against her skin, she smiled softly.

They were building the world they used to dream of.

And she was part of it.

Epilogue

A New Internet, A New World, A New You

The transformation unfolding before us is far more than a technological shift. It is a philosophical revolution—one that challenges the foundations of ownership, governance, identity, work, creativity, finance, and human connection. Web 3.0 is not merely changing the internet; it is changing what it means to participate in the digital world. As you reach the end of this book, you are not simply more informed—you are now part of the next evolution of global innovation. You have learned how decentralized systems unlock new freedoms, new opportunities, and new structures for digital life. You have seen how individuals around the world are reinventing how they work, create, collaborate, and thrive. And now, you stand at the gateway of a future where you have full control over your identity, your assets, your reputation, and your destiny.

The most powerful truth about Web 3.0 is that it is built by the people who believe in it. The decentralized economy does not rely on tech giants, banks, or government structures to function. It relies on creators, contributors, builders, dreamers, and ordinary individuals who recognize the value of a user-owned digital world. This means that you—no matter your background, age, experience level, or location—have a role to play. Some will build decentralized applications that transform industries. Others will create art, music, brands, or educational content powered by NFTs or digital ownership. Some will join DAOs, help make decisions, and guide the direction of global communities. Others will invest, stake, provide liquidity, or curate digital experiences. Every contribution, big or small, shapes the future of Web 3.0.

The most transformative opportunities of the coming decade will not belong to the people who simply observe this movement—they will belong to those who participate early and contribute consistently. The decentralized internet is open. It is permissionless. It does not ask for a résumé. It does not care about degrees, titles, or status. It rewards effort, creativity, and authentic contribution. Your on-chain reputation—the history of your verifiable actions—becomes your key to future opportunities. You earn trust not by who you know, but by what you do. And every interaction you make strengthens your digital presence in ways no traditional system can replicate.

We are approaching a world where digital identity is sovereign, where financial systems operate without borders, where global communities govern themselves transparently, and where creativity becomes a form of ownership that generates lifelong value. Blockchain technology, DAOs, decentralized identity, metaverse ecosystems, and interoperable assets are constructing an entirely new digital civilization—one in which individuals hold unprecedented power. You are living through the early chapters of history that future generations will study as the turning point of the digital age.

Yet, with great freedom comes responsibility. Web 3.0 requires personal stewardship. It demands that you safeguard your digital identity, understand the mechanics of decentralized systems, and make informed choices. The more you learn, the more protected and empowered you become. This journey is not about perfection. It is about progress—one wallet connection, one DAO vote, one on-chain action at a time.

You have the opportunity to become a digital pioneer in a world that is still unfolding. The people who thrive in Web 3.0 are those who experiment, explore, and remain curious. They test new platforms, join communities, create projects, and collaborate across borders. They understand that the decentralized internet is still young—and that early adopters are building the foundation for the next generation. They know that the world is changing, and instead of resisting it, they embrace it.

As you move forward, remember that Web 3.0 is not a destination but an evolution. It will continue to expand, adapt, and reinvent itself. New protocols will emerge. New industries will form. New opportunities will appear faster than ever before. And you will have the chance to shape that future instead of watching from the sidelines. Whether you want to build wealth, create art, launch businesses, join global communities, or simply protect your digital identity, Web 3.0 offers infinite possibilities. The only limit is your willingness to begin.

The decentralized world belongs to its participants. And now that you have the knowledge, the tools, and the vision—you are ready to take your place in it. The new internet is here. The new economy is forming. The new digital society is rising. And the next chapter is yours to write.

Welcome to the future. Welcome to Web 3.0.

www.ingramcontent.com/pod-product-compliance
Lightning Source LLC
LaVergne TN
LVHW022009200926
848481LV00007B/2306
9798295491061